THE LEBRETON GALLERY

THE MILITARY TECHNOLOGY COLLECTION
OF THE CANADIAN WAR MUSEUM

Andrew Burtch and Jeff Noakes

D1567972

CANADIAN WAR MUSEUM
MUSÉE CANADIEN DE LA GUERRE

Library and Archives Canada
Cataloguing in Publication

Burtch, Andrew
The LeBreton Gallery: the military technology
collection of the Canadian War Museum /
Andrew Burtch and Jeff Noakes.

(Souvenir catalogue series, 2291-6385)
Issued also in French under title:
La galerie LeBreton : la collection de matériel
militaire du Musée canadien de la guerre.
ISBN 978-0-660-20309-6
Cat. no.: NM23-5/11-2015E

1. LeBreton Gallery (Canada).
2. Military museums – Canada.
3. Canada – History, Military – Museums.
4. Canada. Canadian Armed Forces – History.
5. Canada – Armed Forces – History.
I. Noakes, Jeffrey.
II. Canadian War Museum.
III. Title.
IV. Series: Souvenir catalogue series.

U13 C32 O88 2015
355.0074'71
C2014-980056-8

Published by the
Canadian War Museum
1 Vimy Place
Ottawa, ON K1A 0M8
warmuseum.ca

Printed and bound in Canada.

Published in association with the
Friends of the Canadian War Museum.

Cover image:
Six-Ton Tank M1917 / CWM19980143-001

Souvenir Catalogue series, 10
ISSN 2291-6385

CONTENTS

4   A Message from the Friends
    of the Canadian War Museum

8   Foreword

11 History of the Collection

21 Transport and Supply

31 Engineering and Maintenance

37 Command and Communications

47 Fighting Vehicles

63 Air

73 Sea

85 Cannons and Mortars

91 Field Artillery and Howitzers

101 Anti-Aircraft and Anti-Tank Guns

109 Rockets and Missiles

A MESSAGE FROM THE FRIENDS OF THE CANADIAN WAR MUSEUM

The Friends of the Canadian War Museum is pleased and proud to have provided the funding for this catalogue highlighting the collection of large military and naval weapons, vehicles and other equipment on display in the Museum's LeBreton Gallery.

The Gallery was initially used as storage space for some of the Museum's larger artifacts that were not integrated into its permanent exhibitions. Open to the public, it soon became one of the more popular galleries for visitors. As its popularity grew, so did demands for information about the equipment on display and its significance to Canadian military history.

In 2013, the Museum reorganized the artifacts in the LeBreton Gallery to acknowledge and formalize the learning opportunities represented by the equipment in which visitors had shown so much interest. At the time, attention was given to highlighting aspects of the Museum's naval and air technology collection. As a former naval officer, I was delighted that space had been found to display the gigantic variable depth sonar body, a technology just coming into service when I was at sea.

The Museum preserves this collection so that the public can better understand the technology that Canadians have used, faced and experienced in times of peace and conflict. The collection presents a wide variety of equipment used in warfare over the past 300 years. Each piece tells us something about the human ingenuity and intent behind its creation and use, as well as the individual's experience of coming face to face with it.

The involvement of the Friends in the Gallery goes beyond producing this catalogue and providing guide interpreters to explain the collection to visitors. The Friends has also helped fund the acquisition and restoration of many pieces on display, and its members are among the volunteers who work on maintaining and restoring the equipment.

The Friends is an all-volunteer group that in 1985 conceived and spearheaded the "Passing the Torch" campaign, which raised almost $18 million for the design and development of exhibits and displays

for the new Canadian War Museum. Subsequently, the group has directly donated more than $1 million for projects that enrich the visitor experience and enhance the Museum's collection.

Museum visitors encounter the Friends as volunteer interpreters — many of them veterans — in the Museum's galleries. Visitors also benefit from our support to Museum projects involving acquisition, archiving, education, research, conservation and restoration of artifacts.

A registered not-for-profit charity, the Friends welcomes donations to support this magnificent national institution. You may join the Friends of the Canadian War Museum from anywhere and at any age, to get involved and stay informed about developments at the Museum. If you are interested in learning more, please go to our website at www.friends-amis.org, visit our Facebook page or call 819-776-8618.

Douglas Rowland, C.D.
Past President,
Friends of the
Canadian War Museum

FOREWORD

The Canadian War Museum's LeBreton Gallery contains the most extensive collection of military technology in Canada. Its displays feature a wide variety of weapons, vehicles and other equipment used by Canadians, their allies and opposing forces in military conflicts from the 18th century to the present.

The Museum preserves this collection of large military weapons, vehicles and equipment so that the public can better understand the technology that Canadians have operated or confronted in times of peace and conflict.

This companion publication highlights 39 artifacts from the Museum's technology collection. Representative of the larger collection on display in the Gallery, the catalogue features transport vehicles, armoured fighting vehicles, an aircraft, missiles, torpedoes and naval guns, as well as artillery that includes field guns, howitzers and trench mortars.

Conflict shaped this technology, and some pieces played a winning role in battle. The basic objectives underlying armed conflict remain largely unchanged — to attack, to protect and to kill — but the means of achieving these goals have evolved dramatically over time.

On a more fundamental level, this collection of technology tells stories of the human experience of war. The artifacts on display are not inert hunks of metal, rubber and wood but, rather, they represent tools used by thousands of military personnel in peace and in war. Some are intrinsically linked to an individual soldier's story, while others can help visitors understand the scale and experience of industrialized warfare.

The LeBreton Gallery is one of the Museum's most popular destinations, visited frequently by adults, intergenerational groups and young families who appreciate its wide open spaces. Museum volunteers, many of whom are veterans, are often present in the Gallery to share their lived experience with visitors.

The Gallery is a multi-purpose space. A popular venue for banquets, receptions, concerts and other special events, it hosts a wide range of people who might not otherwise have occasion to visit the Museum.

As someone who was deeply involved in the development of the Military Technology Collection over the course of my career, it is my hope that readers will enjoy the overview of the LeBreton Gallery in the pages that follow.

This souvenir catalogue would not have been possible without the generous support of the Friends of the Canadian War Museum. The Friends' 700-plus members have a passion for preserving and sharing the legacy of generations of Canadians who fought for their country. To all of them, I extend the Museum's sincerest thanks.

James Whitham
Director General,
Canadian War Museum
and Vice-President,
Canadian Museum of History

HISTORY OF THE COLLECTION

The history of the technology collection is also a history of the Canadian War Museum itself. The Museum dates back to 1880, when the Militia Headquarters in Ottawa began to collect artifacts and archival materials related to Canada's military history.

The collection grew exponentially during the First World War. At that time, Dominion Archivist Arthur Doughty identified the need to preserve artifacts from the war. Securing support from the Canadian government, he arranged to bring to Canada German weapons captured as trophies by Canadians, as well as contributions from Canada's allies. He organized the first travelling exhibition of this material in 1916.

While in England in 1917 to organize Canada's archival record of the war, Doughty also arranged to have new collections of weapons assembled for travel across North America. Between 1917 and 1920 — particularly after the war had ended — these exhibitions attracted large and enthusiastic crowds. Visitors were exhorted to celebrate victory by looking at the "weapons and instruments used by our boys and against our boys in their supreme struggle which, after four years, ended in a complete victory."

In December 1918, the Canadian government established the Commission on War Records and Trophies to distribute captured enemy materials and representative Allied equipment that could be used in memorials across Canada. Under the direction of Arthur Doughty, the Commission saved a number of artifacts in the hope that they would eventually be displayed in a museum. In the interim, they were housed in a newly constructed temporary building situated beside the Dominion Archives facility at 330 Sussex Drive in Ottawa, in what was known as the Trophies Building.

After the outbreak of the Second World War, numerous trophies and artifacts across the country were scrapped to help provide materials for the war effort. Many of the items scrapped in Ottawa had been set aside for the planned Canadian War Museum, an institution that formally opened in 1942.

Following the German surrender in 1945, the "First Canadian War Museum Collection Team," instigated and commanded by Captain Farley Mowat, traversed the Netherlands and Allied-occupied Germany. This unofficial unit collected hundreds of tons of German military equipment, and arranged for its transport back to Canada. Part of this collection made its way to the Museum, and some of these pieces are on display in its galleries.

From 1945 to the 1980s, the Museum's technology collection gradually grew, taking advantage of offers from the Department of National Defence to transfer obsolete equipment to the Museum's care.

Heading into the 1990s, the collection received gifts of material from the former Soviet Union, Ukraine and Germany. Museum specialists also sought out important artifacts in private collections and other museums to expand the Museum's holdings, as well as to address gaps in its collection.

While the technology collection became increasingly impressive, its accommodation remained far from ideal. In June 1967, the Museum moved into the former home of the Public Archives of Canada. Much of the collection remained on display next door in the Trophies Building, which had been renamed the Annex. The artifacts remained there until 1983, when the Annex

was demolished to make room for the new National Gallery of Canada. At this point, the Museum's entire holdings, including the technology collection, were housed in Vimy House, a storage facility and occasional display area. In September 2003, the facility was closed to the public and the Museum's National Collection was carefully transferred to its current location at LeBreton Flats.

Today, much of the Museum's large and impressive technology collection is displayed in the LeBreton Gallery, a modern, climate-controlled facility linked to a workshop and collections vaults. This large, open space, overlooked by a mezzanine, gives visitors the opportunity to appreciate the scope and scale of the collection. The Canadian War Museum is proud to preserve this world-class collection for the benefit of its visitors and for all Canadians.

STORY OF AN ARTIFACT:
SIX-TON TANK M1917

The Museum's Six-Ton Tank M1917 is one of only two remaining examples in Canada. One of nearly a thousand manufactured in the United States after it joined the First World War in 1917, the M1917 was based on the French Renault FT light tank. The war ended just as the M1917 entered production, and none made it to the battlefields of Europe.

Six-Ton Tank M1917
Used by Canada, 1940–1943

CANADIANS AND THE M1917

In 1940, Canada's Colonel F. F. Worthington, a long-time advocate for a Canadian armoured fighting capability and the father of the Canadian Armoured Corps (now the Royal Canadian Armoured Corps), arranged for the acquisition of approximately 250 American-made M1917s. They came to Canada as "scrap metal" from the then-neutral United States for use as training vehicles. Although slow and unreliable, they proved useful until newer tanks became available beginning in 1943.

LIFE AS A TRACTOR

The Museum's M1917 was last used as a tractor in a logging operation near Bracebridge, Ontario.

The rusting hulk that the Museum acquired in 1997 bore little resemblance to the original tank. Sold for surplus, it had been stripped of its turret and parts of its hull. The revitalization of this rare vehicle required 4 years of extensive effort and the support of Richard Iorweth Thorman, the Friends of the Canadian War Museum and DEW Engineering. The restoration included construction of a new upper hull and turret.

TRANSPORT AND SUPPLY

War has a big appetite — militaries go through tons of ammunition, fuel and food every day. Forces in battle and on the move must have these essentials supplied continually if they are to keep operating and fighting.

General Service Wagon Mk III

Used by Canada, 1916–1918

GENERAL SERVICE WAGON

During the First World War, simple wooden wagons carried food, ammunition and equipment from railheads toward the trenches in long supply lines.

The Canadian Expeditionary Force relied on thousands of draught and pack animals to pull wagons and artillery pieces, and to carry supplies. Wagons travelled day and night to keep the troops fighting, and were often targeted by enemy fire.

The Canadian firm Massey-Harris manufactured this wagon in Toronto in 1916. After the war, many service wagons, including this one, were sold at auction to local farmers. Its British owners donated it to the Museum in 1968.

EMERGENCY FOOD VAN

The British adapted civilian Fordson (Ford of England) E83W vans to serve as mobile canteens during the Second World War.

This van was the first of a series paid for by Commonwealth organizations and donated to the British government. Volunteers staffed the vans, serving more than 7.5 million meals during the war.

R.H. Patterson & Co. Ltd., the Ford dealership in Newcastle upon Tyne, England, that adopted this van, is still operating today.

The Friends of the Canadian War Museum helped finance the acquisition and restoration of the vehicle, in addition to contributing their time and labour.

Emergency Food Van No. 1 E83W
Used by the United Kingdom, 1941–1945

ILTIS LIGHT UTILITY VEHICLE

"As we came around to the town, the headlights lit up on a group of about 25 Serbs, and they're all armed and waving for us to stop."

Master Corporal John Tescione

Canadian soldiers Private Phillip Badanai and Master Corporal John Tescione drove this Iltis in Croatia on New Year's Eve, 1994. They were serving with UNPROFOR, a United Nations mission in the former Yugoslavia. Serbian troops fired on their vehicle when they passed through a Serb-held town. Badanai suffered two bullet wounds to the back, and Tescione received six to his head and arms. They survived a harrowing 20-kilometre drive to their battalion headquarters. Badanai, the driver, was awarded the Meritorious Service Medal, and named Peacekeeper of the Year by the Canadian Citizenship Federation in 1995.

"We were driving through . . . but the next thing you know all the weapons were cocked, and we're not even through the crowd yet and they started opening fire."

Private Phillip Badanai

Light Utility Vehicle Wheeled (Iltis)

Used by Canada, 1984–2004

G-WAGEN

Light Utility Vehicle, Wheeled, Command and Reconnaissance

Used by Canada, 2004 – Present

Canadian soldiers began using the Mercedes-Benz Gelandewagen, or G-Wagen, on patrols in Afghanistan in 2004. The G-Wagens replaced aging Iltis vehicles.

On December 12, 2005 Afghan insurgents detonated an improvised explosive device (IED) near this G-Wagen, commanded by Captain Manuel Panchana-Moya,

90 kilometres outside Kandahar, Afghanistan. Injured in the blast were Panchana-Moya, Private Ryan Crawford, Private Russell Murdock and Tim Albone, an embedded British journalist. The armour fitted to the vehicle saved their lives. Insurgents increased the size and effectiveness of their IEDs in subsequent attacks.

RETRIEVAL

An American Chinook
helicopter delivers the
damaged G-Wagen to
the Kandahar Airfield
after the attack.

ENGINEERING AND MAINTENANCE

If something can go wrong, it probably will. Recovery and engineering vehicles keep forces on the move by helping to repair bridges and prepare fortifications, and by recovering, repairing and maintaining vehicles.

GREAT EASTERN RAMP

This rare vehicle is one of ten Churchill tanks converted by the Royal Engineers to become a "Great Eastern Ramp": an engineering assault vehicle. It was designed to deploy a heavy roadway so that other vehicles could drive over obstacles.

This example is one of two Great Eastern Ramps sent to Canada for testing in 1946. The Museum purchased the vehicle from a scrapyard in Kemptville, Ontario, in 1972.

Mk IV RE Great Eastern Ramp

Used by the United Kingdom, 1944–1945

DIAMOND T MACHINERY TRUCK

During the Second World War, Canadians used well-equipped mobile workshops to repair and refurbish vehicle equipment and components.

This truck was a self-contained workshop, with workbenches that folded down from both sides and a generator to supply electrical power for its operations. Its wide range of equipment included machine tools for working with metal, an air compressor for spray-painting, and repair and charging equipment for vehicle batteries. Skilled technicians used this equipment to repair damaged and worn parts so that vehicles could continue operating.

During the war, the Canadian automotive industry made hundreds of thousands of vehicles. However, all trucks with a capacity greater than 3 tons were still acquired from foreign manufacturers, such as Diamond T in Chicago, Illinois.

Diamond T Type "M" Machinery Truck, Model 975A

Used by Canada, 1941–1950s

COMMAND AND COMMUNICATIONS

Command and communication vehicles are an armed force's brain and nervous system. They help commanders transmit orders, relay information and coordinate operations.

HARLEY-DAVIDSON WLC

The Harley-Davidson WLC (WL for its engine type, C for Canadian) was often used for communications in wartime, largely by despatch riders carrying messages and documents. It was also used by military police. The WLC model was used in Canada and overseas in the Second World War and the Korean War.

Almost one-quarter of the 88,000 Harley-Davidson motorcycles produced during the Second World War were built to Canadian specifications.

Post-war consumers in North America, many of them former soldiers, were eager to purchase surplus Harley-Davidsons for use in civilian life.

Harley-Davidson Motorcycle, Model WLC

Used by Canada, 1942–1956

HEAVY UTILITY PERSONNEL COMMAND CAR

During the Second World War, Canada produced more than 400,000 Canadian Military Pattern (CMP) trucks. The heavy utility personnel (HUP) vehicle was one of many types of CMP trucks. Manufactured by Ford Motor Company of Canada and General Motors of Canada, the CMP's standardized design allowed for a faster rate of production and easier maintenance in the field.

The C8A HUP was introduced in 1942. It was the only CMP model manufactured solely by General Motors of Canada. The company built 12,967 HUPs during the Second World War.

The Museum's CMP C8A served as a personnel transport during the war.

CMP C8A 1C1 Heavy Utility Personnel Vehicle

Used by Canada, 1942–1945

LIEUTENANT-GENERAL H. D. G. CRERAR'S CARAVAN

Lieutenant-General H. D. G. (Harry) Crerar, commander of the First Canadian Army in 1944–1945, used this trailer as a mobile office.

The trailer was the heart of Crerar's headquarters from the D-Day landings in Normandy until the end of the war, after which it was brought to Canada. The trailer held a desk, maps, a conference table and telephones. Crerar hosted fellow generals and important guests in this trailer, including British Prime Minister Winston Churchill. A separate vehicle, a 4-ton Diamond T truck, towed the trailer and served as Crerar's personal quarters.

3/4-ton Office Trailer

Used by Canada, 1944–1945

SIR HAROLD ALEXANDER'S STAFF CAR

This vehicle was British Field Marshal Sir Harold Alexander's personal staff car during his campaigns in North Africa and Italy during the Second World War. Canadian formations in Italy fought under Alexander's command.

The Ford Motor Company of Canada manufactured this type of vehicle to British standards for use as a specialized command car.

Alexander's command car travelled more than 290,000 kilometres and underwent field modifications and three engine changes during its career. After the war, Alexander — by this time Viscount Alexander of Tunis and Errigal, in recognition of his wartime accomplishments — served as Governor General of Canada from 1946 to 1952.

C11AD Staff Car

Used by the United Kingdom, 1942–1945

Alexander in the Field

Sir Harold Alexander (left) and his driver Sergeant Joseph Wells (right) at the United States Army's Fifth Army Headquarters in Italy, February 1944. Wells, an Ottawa native, served as Alexander's driver from 1939 to 1952.

FIGHTING VEHICLES

A military's principal task in war is combat. In peace, it is to be prepared for combat. Canada, its allies and its enemies have used a wide range of equipment to fight on the ground, at sea and in the air.

PANZER V PANTHER

After invading the Soviet Union in June 1941, German forces suffered heavy losses from Soviet tanks such as the T-34. The Germans responded by developing the tough Panzer V Panther. Its powerful, accurate gun could destroy Allied Sherman tanks from more than a kilometre away.

The Museum's tank was captured, transported to Canada, and then shown in Ottawa during May 1945 victory celebrations. Later displayed at Canadian Forces Base Borden, near Barrie, Ontario, it was transferred to the Canadian War Museum by the Department of National Defence in 2005. Museum staff and volunteers dedicated 4,000 hours to the Panther's restoration.

Panzerkampfwagen V Panther Ausf A

Used by Germany, 1943–1945

T-34/85 TANK

One of the most successful tanks ever constructed, the Soviet Union's T-34/85 was inexpensive and mechanically reliable. It combined heavy armour with a powerful gun.

Early models of the T-34 generally outclassed German tanks. When Germany introduced more powerful tanks and anti-tank guns in response, the Soviet Union countered by upgrading to the T-34/85. The Soviet Union and other countries produced tens of thousands of this model during and after the Second World War.

This tank was built in Nizhny Tagil, in the Soviet Union, in 1944, and saw action in Ukraine. The Soviet government donated it to the Canadian War Museum in 1988.

T-34/85 Tank

Used by the Soviet Union, 1943/44–1960s

VALENTINE TANK

The Soviet Union used the British-designed, Canadian-manufactured Valentine tank during the Second World War. The Canadian Pacific Railway's Angus Shops in Montréal made 1,420 Valentines. Canada shipped all but 30 of them to the Soviet army.

During a Soviet offensive in Ukraine in January 1944, this Valentine broke through the ice covering a swampy river. All three crew members escaped, but the tank sank out of sight. Forty-six years later, residents of the nearby village of Telepino recovered it. In 1992, the government of Ukraine gave this tank to the Canadian War Museum.

Valentine Mk VIIA Tank

Used by the Soviet Union, 1943–1944

UNIVERSAL CARRIER MK II*

Canadian and Allied forces made extensive use of the multi-purpose Universal Carrier. Often called a "Bren Gun Carrier" after the light machine gun of that name, it could be fitted with a range of weapons, including machine guns, mortars, light anti-tank guns or flamethrowers. It could also tow light artillery or supply trailers, and transport the wounded.

The Ford Motor Company of Canada and the Dominion Bridge Company made some 29,000 Mk II Universal Carriers during the Second World War.

The Museum's carrier, built in 1944, was the last to serve in the Canadian military before the transition to the M113 series of armoured personnel carriers in the 1960s. The Department of National Defence refurbished it before presenting it to the Museum in 1968.

Universal Carrier No. 2 Mk II*

Used by Canada, 1944–1961

M113 ARMOURED PERSONNEL CARRIER

The Canadian government ordered American M113 armoured personnel carriers (APCs) in 1963 to increase the mobility and protection of infantry battalions in Germany during the Cold War. The Museum's M113 APC was the first the Canadian Army received in 1964. In 1992, Canadian soldiers transported it from Germany to Sarajevo to join the United Nations mission in the former Yugoslavia. An anti-tank mine severely damaged it during a patrol in 1994. In recognition of its 30 years in service, the Electrical and Mechanical Engineering Branch of the Canadian Armed Forces restored this vehicle to its present state.

M113A2 Armoured Personnel Carrier

Used by Canada, 1964–1994

RAM KANGAROO

The Ram Kangaroo entered service during the Second World War as one of the first armoured personnel carriers.

Canadian Lieutenant-General Guy Simonds devised the "Kangaroo" in August 1944. As he prepared for a new phase in the Normandy Campaign, he looked for a means to protect soldiers from bullets and shrapnel while they were being transported to their deployment points. His solution was to remove the turret from a tank, which opened up space for 12 soldiers. The resulting vehicles were nicknamed "Kangaroos" after the code name of the Canadian workshop that created the first example.

The first Kangaroos were made by removing the main armament from M7 Priest self-propelled guns. The majority of the Kangaroos used during the war were converted Ram tanks, like the Museum's example. They worked so well that the Canadians and the British used Ram Kangaroos in every major battle until the end of the war.

Richard Iorweth Thorman and the Friends of the Canadian War Museum helped finance the restoration of this vehicle, and the Friends also provided time and labour.

Ram Kangaroo Armoured Personnel Carrier

Used by Canada, 1944–1945

LEOPARD C2 TANK

Variants of the German-made Leopard have served as Canada's main battle tank since the late 1970s.

The Leopard C2 is an upgrade of the original Leopard C1, developed as a response to the introduction of new Soviet tanks starting in the 1970s and 1980s.

Turrets from more modern German Leopards provided improved targeting systems for the tank's weapons. The addition of armour improved protection for its crew. Canadians used Leopard C2s in combat for the first time between 2007 and 2011, to support operations in Kandahar, Afghanistan.

Leopard C2 Tank

Used by Canada, 1999 – Present

AIR

In the 20th century, aircraft were developed as a means for military forces to seize control of the air for observation, attack, defence and transportation.

CF-101 VOODOO

The CF-101 Voodoo interceptor helped guard North American skies for more than 20 years.

The first Voodoos, acquired in 1961, replaced older CF-100 interceptors after the CF-105 Avro Arrow — originally intended to replace them — was cancelled. The high-speed, long-range Voodoo, capable of operating in all types of weather, was designed to intercept, identify and, if necessary, attack aircraft flying in North American skies. A link to the SAGE (Semi-Automatic Ground Environment) computer network helped guide the aircraft to its target, which it could attack with heat-seeking Falcon missiles and nuclear-tipped Genie rockets. The Museum's aircraft is a CF-101F, which had two sets of flying controls to help train aircrew.

CF-101 Voodoo

Used by Canada, 1961–1987

CLOSE ESCORT

As part of their air defence role, Voodoos would intercept, identify and accompany Soviet reconnaissance and patrol aircraft flying near Canadian airspace.

This CF-101 is escorting a Soviet Bear bomber in 1985, near the end of the Voodoo's Canadian service career.

AIR-TO-AIR MISSILES: AIM-4D FALCON AND AIM-9B SIDEWINDER

The AIM-4D Falcon and AIM-9B Sidewinder air-to-air missiles were guided by the infrared (heat) radiation their targets emitted.

Despite its disappointing performance in air-to-air combat between fighter aircraft, the AIM-4D Falcon remained in service with the Canadian and U.S. air forces. Interceptor aircraft like the CF-101 Voodoo carried them to use against larger, slower and less manoeuverable Soviet bombers.

The Museum's AIM-9B Sidewinder missile is a training version. It was likely used by the Royal Canadian Navy, whose Banshee fighters carried the Sidewinder between 1958 and 1962. Early versions of the missile, like this one, were only effective from behind a target aircraft, where the heat of its exhaust and engine were easiest to pick up. Newer versions can home in on a target from any angle.

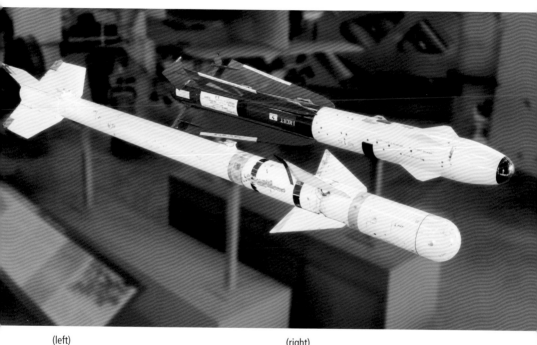

(left)

AIM-9B Sidewinder Air-to-Air Missile

Used by Canada, 1958–1960s

(right)

AIM-4D Falcon Air-to-Air Missile

Used by Canada, 1960s–1980s

AERIAL BOMBS

As air combat evolved during the First World War, Britain's Royal Flying Corps began to use incendiary bombs (top) and 20-pound Cooper bombs (bottom).

The incendiary bomb used a highly flammable chemical mixture to spark fires. These fires could cause even more destruction than the high explosives in regular bombs, especially in dense target areas like cities, warehouses and factories. Incendiary bombs were used to devastating effect during the Second World War.

The Cooper bomb was small and light enough to be carried by fighter aircraft as well as by bombers. Designed to create high-velocity fragments on detonation, the Cooper bomb was used against troops, road transport, airfields and other targets in the open. As the First World War progressed, Allied and German aircraft attacked ground targets at or near the front lines more and more frequently, using machine gun fire and bombs like this one.

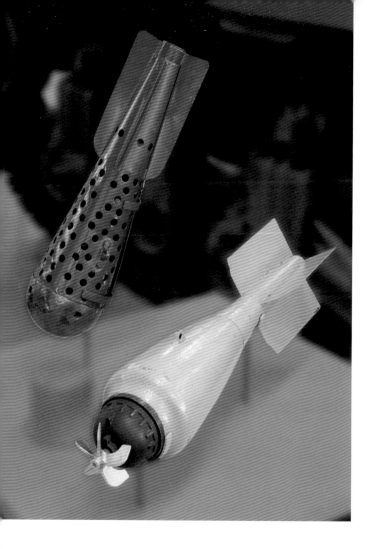

(top)

Mk I Incendiary Carcass Bomb

Used by Great Britain, 1914 – around 1918

(bottom)

20-Pound Cooper Mk I High Explosive Bomb

Used by Great Britain, 1916–1930s

SEA

Because much of the world is covered by water, the warship is one of the oldest and most powerful weapon systems in the world. The following artifacts were used by ships to attack or defend against threats at sea, underwater or in the air.

WEATHER STATION "KURT"

In October 1943, during the Second World War, armed German sailors installed this automated weather station, called "Kurt," in northern Labrador.

Weather forecasting is vital for planning military operations at sea, on land and in the air, and Kurt was intended to help predict conditions over the North Atlantic and Europe. After a short period of operation, however, the Germans were no longer able to receive its signals.

Germany established a number of northern weather stations, but Kurt was the only one installed in North America.

**Weather Station,
Land, Automated,
WFL (*Wetterfunkgerät
Land*) 26**

Used by Germany, 1943

WEATHER STATION "KURT" INSTALLED

This German photograph shows Kurt following its installation. To conceal the station's origins, one cylinder is labelled "Canadian Meteor Service." The Germans hoped these markings would convince anyone who found the station that it was Canadian government equipment.

WEATHER STATION "KURT" IN 1981

This photograph shows the remains of Kurt in 1981. Most of those who had installed it died during the war, and the story of the station remained virtually unknown until the late 1970s, when a German researcher uncovered evidence of the Labrador operation.

VARIABLE DEPTH SONAR

Canadian ships used Variable Depth Sonar (VDS) to extend the range and accuracy of submarine detection. The Royal Canadian Navy installed this type of sonar on its Iroquois-class destroyers.

Sonar uses sound to detect submarines. It can project pulses of sound and listen for a reflected echo (active sonar). It can also listen for sounds made by submarines (passive sonar). Temperature layers in the water can distort the sonar beam, complicating submarine detection.

Canadian scientists developed the VDS in the 1950s to overcome this challenge. Towed underwater from the stern of a ship, the VDS could detect submarines more effectively than hull-mounted sonar.

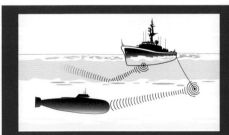

This graphic shows how the Variable Depth Sonar (VDS) works. The sonar beam from a ship's hull-mounted sonar (top) is reflected by a temperature layer in the water, and cannot detect the submarine. The sonar beam from a VDS lowered beneath the temperature layer (bottom) is able to detect the submarine.

AN/SQS-505 Variable Depth Sonar Towed Body

Used by Canada, 1971–1990s

(top)

Torpedo, British, 18-inch, Mk IV

Used by Canada, 1910–1922

(centre)

Mk 14 Mod 3A Torpedo

Used by Canada, 1968–1974

(bottom)

Soviet Type 53 Torpedo

Used by North Korea, 1940s–1950

TORPEDOES

Torpedoes are self-propelled, underwater missiles that can be launched from submarines, surface vessels or aircraft. They are designed to explode upon contact with or near the hull of a surface vessel or submarine. The Museum's collection includes various types of torpedoes.

The **British 18-inch torpedo** (top) was one of the first to be acquired by the Royal Canadian Navy. Part of the armament of the cruiser HMCS (His Majesty's Canadian Ship) *Niobe*, one of the Navy's first two ships, this torpedo complemented the ship's numerous guns.

The **American Mark 14 torpedo** (centre) was used to attack Japanese shipping during the Second World War, and also served the Royal Canadian Navy in submarines based at Esquimalt, British Columbia, in the 1960s and 1970s. It was probably intended for use aboard HMCS *Rainbow*, formerly the USS (United States Ship) *Argonaut*, a Tench-class submarine.

The **Soviet Type 53 torpedo** (bottom) is from the Second World War era. It was probably intended to arm North Korean motor torpedo boats and is likely one of a number discovered by the United States First Marine Division near Wonsan, North Korea, in October 1950. It was captured and brought to Canada for examination and testing.

THE 1 1/4-POUNDER NAVAL GUN

This is one of four guns that formed the main armament of the Canadian Fisheries Protection Service Vessel CGS (Canadian Government Ship) *Canada*.

As part of the Canadian Fisheries Protection Service, the vessel patrolled the east coast searching for American civilian ships fishing illegally in Canadian waters. Because this did not require heavy armament, *Canada* carried four of these relatively light automatic weapons.

1 1/4-Pounder Automatic Gun

Used by Canada, 1905–1910s

CGS CANADA GUN AND CREW

In this photograph taken in Bermuda, some of CGS *Canada*'s crew pose with one of the ship's four "pom-pom" guns. It was often called a "pom-pom" because of the heavy, thumping sound it produced when fired.

CANNONS AND MORTARS

Cannons were developed to fire against ships, troops and fortifications. Mortars were developed for siege warfare, firing projectiles on a high trajectory to attack targets protected by fortifications and usually out of direct sight.

Testing the Conversion

This photograph shows the first cannon converted by the Montréal firm Gilbert & Sons being readied for a test firing in August 1879. The tube used in the conversion process can be seen protruding from the gun's muzzle (right).

THE 32/64-POUNDER PALLISER CANNON

Rising tensions between Great Britain and Russia in 1877–1878 led Canada to upgrade its coastal defences.

A number of 32-pounder smoothbore cannons were removed from fortifications and converted into 64-pounder rifled muzzle-loading guns, using a process developed by Sir William Palliser. The resulting weapons offered greater range and firepower, but contract disputes delayed their completion for 7 years. By then, they were obsolete for use against modern armoured warships.

32/64-Pounder Palliser Converted Rifled Muzzle-Loading Cannon

Used by Canada, conversion in 1887

7.58 cm lMW (*leichter Minenwerfer*) n.A.
Used by Germany, 1916–1918

THE 7.58 CM TRENCH MORTAR

German infantry used *minenwerfer* (mine throwers, or trench mortars) on the front lines during the First World War.

For portability, many trench mortars were designed to be pulled along on their wheels or disassembled into smaller loads, but their short range meant they had to be placed close to the front lines. Germany produced trench mortars in a wide range of sizes; this is one of the smaller models. The 12th Canadian Machine Gun Company captured this mortar, and it was later sent to Canada as a war trophy.

FIELD ARTILLERY AND HOWITZERS

Traditionally, field guns fired projectiles on a low trajectory against targets in the open, while howitzers fired projectiles on a higher trajectory against targets hidden by geography or obstacles.

THE 25-POUNDER FIELD GUN

The 25-pounder, one of the most effective and iconic artillery pieces ever used by the Canadian Army, was Canada's standard field gun during the Second World War and the Korean War.

The British-designed gun offered reliability, firepower and a good range. A circular platform, carried underneath the gun, allowed it to be rotated quickly. More than 17,700 such 25-pounders were manufactured in various Allied countries. Sorel Industries in Sorel, Quebec, made nearly 3,800 guns, including the Museum's example.

The 25-pounders remained in Canadian service until they were replaced by the American 105 mm howitzer in the mid-1950s.

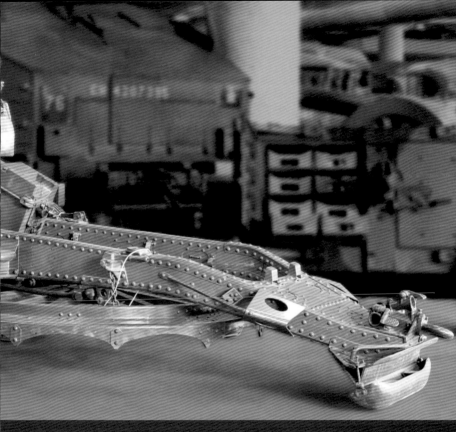

**Quick Firing 25-Pounder
Mk II Field Gun**

Used by Canada, 1939–1956

A 25-POUNDER IN ACTION

Members of the 2nd Field Regiment, Royal Canadian Artillery, engage in an emergency action north of the town of Campobasso, Italy, during the Second World War. The field artillery trailer, which holds ammunition, can be seen on the right.

THE 21 CM *MÖRSER*

This First World War howitzer was one of the most important types of heavy artillery used by the German army.

Although its name is translated as "mortar," the *Mörser* was more like a heavy howitzer, and could destroy trenches and protective dugouts up to 9,400 metres away. The steel "shoes" attached to its wheels helped it traverse rough and muddy terrain. A later version, introduced in 1916, had a longer barrel designed to increase its relatively short range.

The 18th Canadian Infantry Battalion from London, Ontario, captured this gun. The Commission on War Records and Trophies allocated it to Hamilton, Ontario, where it remained on display until it was donated to the Canadian War Museum in 1994.

21 cm *Mörser* 10
Used by Germany, 1910–1918

C1 M114 155 MM HOWITZER

Howitzers provided artillery support for Canadian forces during the Cold War.

In service from the mid-1950s, these American-designed howitzers were built under licence in Canada for the Canadian military and other North Atlantic Treaty Organization (NATO) countries.

The Museum's gun served from 1958 until 1966, and fired more than 1,600 rounds during that time. Beginning in 1968, the Canadian Army replaced the 155s in Europe with M109 self-propelled guns.

Loading a 155

Canadian gunners load a 155 mm howitzer while on a training exercise. A long rod, called a rammer, is being used to push the projectile and propellant charge into place.

C1 M114 155 mm Howitzer

Used by Canada, 1954–1970

ANTI-AIRCRAFT AND ANTI-TANK GUNS

These weapons were created to defend against 20th century military threats — aircraft and tanks.

A 6-POUNDER IN ACTION

A 6-pounder fires on a German position during fighting in the town of Ortona, Italy, on December 21, 1943, during the Second World War.

THE 6-POUNDER ANTI-TANK GUN

6-Pounder
Anti-Tank Gun Mk 1
Used by Canada, 1942–1957

Canadian, British and other Commonwealth forces used the 6-pounder anti-tank gun during and after the Second World War.

Although it became less effective as more heavily armoured German tanks appeared on the battlefield, the 6-pounder remained useful at shorter ranges. A relatively small and light gun, it could be moved forward by its crew to support the infantry and protect against enemy tank attacks. Gunners used the 6-pounder to destroy pillboxes and other fortifications, especially during urban combat.

M38A1 WITH 106 MM RECOILLESS RIFLE

The Museum's M38A1, an upgraded version of the 1940s Jeep, carries a 106 mm recoilless rifle that could be used against tanks and other targets.

When fired, the 106 mm recoilless rifle created a large cloud of smoke, dust and flame, which gave away the gun's position.

Mounting this weapon on a vehicle greatly increased its mobility and allowed soldiers to move quickly after firing. During the Cold War, Canadian soldiers trained to "shoot and scoot," relocating rapidly after firing to escape enemy retaliation.

Anti-Tank Defence
Private Gilles Gaudet (right) of 1 Commando, Canadian Airborne Regiment, loads one of the jeep-mounted 106 mm recoilless rifles deployed in July 1974, at the airport in Nicosia, Cyprus.

M38A1 Utility Vehicle with 106 mm Recoilless Rifle

Used by Canada, 1952–1975 (M38A1); 1950s–1988 (106-mm)

THE 13-POUNDER ANTI-AIRCRAFT GUN

The 13-pounder anti-aircraft gun was developed by the British to counter the new and growing threat of enemy aircraft, and entered into service in November 1915. A liner or sleeve was inserted into the breech and barrel of an 18-pounder gun, allowing it to fire the smaller 13-pounder shell while still using the larger cartridge and propellant charge. This modification increased the velocity of the shells fired from the weapon, which could reach aircraft flying at up to 5,700 metres.

The Museum's gun was one of ten acquired by Canada at the end of the First World War. At the outbreak of the Second World War, it was one of the few anti-aircraft guns in service in Canada.

On the Western Front
Gunners run towards 13-pounders during the First World War. The gun's pedestal mounting allowed it to be aimed upwards at high angles, and it could be attached to a truck or permanent concrete pad.

13-Pounder 9 cwt Anti-Aircraft Gun

Used by Canada, 1918–1942

ROCKETS AND MISSILES

Rockets and missiles deliver warheads without the need for heavy firing equipment, providing more destructive effect from a smaller weapon.

LAND MATTRESS

This is the only surviving example of the Canadian-developed Land Mattress rocket launcher. In late 1944, the Canadian Army completed its development based on a British concept.

Similar rocket launchers named Sea Mattresses were used on landing craft during the 1944 invasion of Normandy, so the Canadian rocket launcher was named the Land Service Mattress, or Land Mattress. One launcher could provide a greater concentration of fire more quickly — 30 rockets in 7.25 seconds — than the Canadian 25-pounder gun, but took much longer to reload.

**Land Mattress
Rocket Launcher**

Used by Canada, 1944–1945

CONTRIBUTIONS

We would like to thank our colleagues on the core exhibition team: Sarah Dobbin, Kathryn Lyons, Michael Miller and Mélanie Morin-Pelletier. Thanks are also due for the hard work of exhibition designer Peter Oulton (oulton + devine), researcher Alexander Comber and interpretive planning consultant Patricia Grimshaw. The collection displayed in the LeBreton Gallery is built on decades of collection, conservation, restoration and research. We also owe a debt of gratitude to many other colleagues and volunteers at the Museum — past and present — as well as to members of the Friends of the Canadian War Museum for their feedback and advice about the Gallery and its development. Assistant Historian Amber Lloydlangston, the Canadian War Museum's photographer Bill Kent and our publications coordinator Lee Wyndham were instrumental in putting together this souvenir catalogue.

Andrew Burtch
Jeff Noakes
Canadian War Museum

PHOTO CREDITS

© Canadian War Museum

p. 9   Steven Darby / IMG2012-0213-0005-Dm

p. 10 George Metcalf Archival Collection / 20020045-2437

p. 13 George Metcalf Archival Collection / 19390002-220

p. 14 William Kent / CWM2014-0075-0001-Dp1

p. 15 William Kent / CWM2013-0051-0005-Dp1

p. 16 19980143-001

p. 22 19680065-001

p. 25 19990029-001

p. 27 19950050-001

p. 28 20060101-001

p. 30 George Metcalf Archival Collection / 20100119-014

p. 32 19720252-001

p. 35 19720076-001

p. 39 19910090-001

p. 41 19950103-004

p. 43 19590017-001

p. 45 (top) 19490003-001

p. 49 20030358-017

p. 51 19880285-001

p. 53 19920195-001

p. 55 19680041-001

p. 57 20030358-018

p. 59 20000230-007

p. 61 20030358-015

p. 62 George Metcalf Archival Collection / 19930012-304

p. 65 20040061-001

p. 69 (left) 19700011-001 / (right) 19850301-002

p. 71 (top) 19880001-688 / (bottom) 19390002-686

p. 75 19820219-001

p. 76 20030149-001#5

p. 77 20030149-001#8

p. 79 20090085-001

p. 80 (top) 19390001-181 / (centre) 19750076-001 / (bottom) 19600007-001

p. 82 19440021-001

p. 84 George Metcalf Archival Collection / 19940001-214

p. 87 19850408-001

p. 88 19390001-650